Sell Your House For More

10 Essential Steps
From Preparation to Presentation

Mamta Sahota & Vick Sahota

Sell Your House for More

www.SellWithVick.com

Publisher
10-10-10 Publishing
Markham, ON
Canada

Printed in Canada and the United States of America

Table of Contents

Dedication

We dedicate this book to all home sellers who are facing it with curiosity and open-mindedness.

And, of course, we dedicate this book to our lovely children, Reva and Aarav.

Acknowledgements

I would like to thank my dad, **Harbans Lal Sahota**, for being a friend, guide, and mentor. By observing him dealing in real estate, I slowly developed my compassion for serving people.

Vick

I would like to thank **Lakhvir Randhawa** for being a great coach and mentor. He is always available for support at the professional and personal level.

Vick

I would like to thank my dad, **Vijay Kumar Demaney,** for being my closest friend. He is always so confident about my ability to perform better every time. I am so blessed to be his daughter.

Mamta

I would like to thank **Raymond Aaron** for his constant motivation. I have seen a huge change in my life by thinking and talking positive. He has taught me how to gain confidence and have high energy every moment.

Mamta

We would like to thank **Patricia Jaggernauth**, who has been a great example for us. Her enthusiasm and charismatic personality always motivates us to keep going and do our best, irrespective of weather conditions.

We are really grateful to one of the most amazing persons in the whole world, **Justin Trudeau,** for being the leader of our country. We are so proud to be Canadian. Your love and compassion to serve humanity is a great example for everyone.

Last, but not least, we extend a huge thanks to **Rosa Greco,** our personal book architect, for keeping us on track. Rosa was always there for us and is a fabulous person to work with.

Testimonials

I highly recommend Vick Sahota to first-time buyers and investment buyers. We bought investment property through him; as a real estate agent, he understood our investment needs very well and worked diligently in short listing good investment properties within the location we were interested in. He was patient and full of energy. He accommodated our time limitations, and gave 100%, while ensuring we got a good property without paying too much, especially during a time when there were multiple buyers for each property. After purchasing, he continued to provide help, ensuring we could rent the property from the very first month of acquisition.

Neelima Datt

Mamta is a person with extraordinary strategizing skills, which she implements very well in this world of social media driven marketing. She will always be a great asset, and our secret weapon!

Vishal Ram

Being new to Canada, it would have been difficult to find an apartment without his help. Vick helped us get an apartment that suited us best and in a short duration of time. I would say he's the best realtor, and I would definitely recommend him to anyone who needs to find an apartment.

Tanvee Pathare

Vick Sahota is such a great professional real estate agent; he really goes way beyond his duties to help a client by keeping them on the right track and helping them all the way through the process of buying a home. He is a true professional who makes you feel like family.

Sukhbinder Ahluwalia

Vick sold my house within a week. He and Mamta worked with me for 2 weeks, preparing the house for sale. There were hundreds of showings within a week. I received nine offers for my property. My house was sold for way over the asking price. Thanks Vick and Mamta for your hard work and commitment.

Karamjit Kandhola

Vick is an excellent realtor who is full of energy. He is a fantastic person to work with. Because of his proactive approach, attention to details, and aggressive marketing campaign, my house got sold with multiple offers, at a record breaking price in the neighbourhood.

Tamoor Sajid

About the Authors

Meet Vick Sahota

Vick Sahota is a GTA based realtor with extensive experience in the local real estate market. Vick has a passion for real estate and for helping individuals in all walks of life. Whether it is a bachelor pad, your first home, or upsizing to accommodate a growing family, Vick will use his expertise and experience to make sure you make the right decisions and are satisfied with your transaction. Vick will ensure that you find a home that is the right size, in the right neighborhood, and the right price for your lifestyle.

When it comes to selling a home, Vick implements the concept of a full service realtor. Vick has put together his team of professionals to provide all services under one roof. He prepares customised programs for your house and takes care of all ten steps, starting from preparation to presentation of the house. Vick's unique marketing campaign gives full exposure to your property, which turns into a quick and record breaking sale.

Before entering the real estate market, Vick built a career in marketing and sales. He worked for large, international companies in India and Canada. Vick also gained pertinent business experience during his time in logistics with Wal-Mart Canada. Outside of his professional life, Vick values the community and gives priority to becoming involved and helping others. Vick has provided consultation to families who are trying to assist their loved ones through sponsorships and Visa forms. In addition, Vick provides workshops to new immigrants who are interested in settling down and making the key decision of whether they should rent or buy their first home.

Overall, Vick Sahota is more than just a realtor. He is a hardworking and compassionate individual who will always put your needs first and make sure that you have everything you need in order to find the perfect home.

Meet Mamta Sahota

Mamta Sahota is the owner and president of Your Image Toronto Inc. She is an experienced marketing professional who has provided brand consultancy services at various levels of corporations and community organizations. Her expertise is in the area of developing comprehensive marketing campaigns. This may include business development consultancy, communications, development of a marketing plan, on-line marketing, public relations, and so much more.

Mamta prepares customised real estate marketing campaigns for Vick Sahota Homes. Mamta is taking the lead in providing full exposure to real estate properties with comprehensive marketing campaigns, ranging from newspaper, radio, e-mail, and on-line marketing.

Before entering into the real estate market, Mamta had worked with various Citizenship and Immigration Canada funds projects, serving newcomers to Canada. Mamta has served the city of Mississauga for years.

Overall, Mamta is a great marketer and strategist who loves serving the community. Mamta is passionate to see more and more families enjoying their evenings together under their own roof.

Foreword

Are you thinking about selling your house? If your answer is "yes", then *Sell Your House for More* is a great book for you to start reading.

This book reveals all the secrets of selling a property successfully. Real estate marketing has changed dramatically in the last couple of years and with the advent of online marketing you can reach your potential buyer anywhere in the world. Mamta Sahota and Vick Sahota have done a tremendous job of putting together tedious steps of preparing a property and taking the property to the market in an easy, step-by-step approach. This is a must-have workbook for you to sell your house for more.

Selling a property is a team effort and so many specialists are involved in the process. The markets are now highly competitive and this book will serve as a great guide for you. Mamta and Vick will show you what kind of service you should be expecting from your realtor.

I am very confident that after reading this book and taking desired action, you will be able to sell your house for more.

This book demonstrates a very effective and proven system and the strategies that are provided are now yours to keep.

Raymond Aaron
New York Times Bestselling Author

Chapter 1

It's Not Your Home Anymore
- Vick

> *"The way you live in your home and the way you market and sell your house are two different things."*
> – Barb Schwarz

Hello, and welcome to my book.

You might find the title weird, and may be wondering why I crossed out the word *home* and added the word *house*. Why didn't I simply use the title, *Sell Your House for More?* There is a very strong reason behind this. You lived in this house for years, but now you're planning to sell it; thinking about just giving it away makes your heart sink. Believe me, when you think of selling your house, the most important thing to understand is that you have already given up on your house. The reason could be anything, but this is not your home anymore. Now you understand why I crossed out the word *home* in the title. The fact is: nobody sells their home—people sell houses.

Selling your house for more is the ultimate goal for you. Let's face reality, though; in a sellers' market, your house has more chances to get sold fast, but is it going to get you the record breaking price? Don't you want your house to be sold at the highest price in your neighbourhood? With my years of sales experience, I have come up with a step by step guide to prepare and sell your house for more, with multiple offers. Remember, selling a home is a team effort, and every step in this guide is crucial. These steps are divided into two main headings:

1. Preparing your home for sale
2. Marketing your house for maximum exposure

Sell Your House for More is a practical workbook. As you read this book, you will realize that selling a house is not just posting a *house for sale* sign on your lawn. It is much more than that. In this book, you will learn the essential steps involved in selling a property for more. I have put together a step by step approach to get a *sold* sign on your property in less time, and with more money gained. The entire book is divided into two sections. It will reveal to you all the steps involved, from the preparation to the presentation of your house. You will learn how to detach yourself from your home and how to start thinking like a business person who wants to sell his/her property and get the most out of it. What are the necessary steps required and how do you implement these steps?

Action plan

I know you want to take down notes, and you want to prepare your checklist. To make your job easier, I have provided a full page at the end of each chapter, called *Action Plan*. On this page, you can take down the notes as you read each chapter. You can also create a to-do list for yourself. You might also come up with creative ideas and want to take notes, but you also want to continue to focus on your book, so you can go ahead and take notes on each chapter as you're reading and enjoying this book. If you come across any questions while you're reading this book, you can email me at vick@vicksahotahomes.com, and you can also follow me on my Facebook business page which is Vicksahotahomes.

Reason for selling

You might have lived in this house for years and have enjoyed a number of house parties. You might have raised your kid(s) in this house, and so many good memories are attached to it. Now, you're thinking of selling this house; your reason could be anything. You might be upgrading to a bigger house, or you could be downsizing to a smaller place, but the fact doesn't change that you now want to sell this house. So, let's be practical and take the necessary steps to sell your house for top dollar. I know this is harsh to say, since you have lived in this house, but please accept the reality, my dear friend, that with emotions involved, it will be difficult for you to make practical business decisions. Take it as a business deal in which you have to get maximum benefit. Once you understand the reason, and you accept the reality that you're selling your home, it will be much easier for you and for your realtor to get you a better deal.

Treat it as a project

Now that you have decided and accepted that this is not your home anymore but a house that you have to sell for maximum benefit, let's treat it as a project. For every goal and for every project, there is a deadline. Your deadline could be the date for moving to a new house, so you need to sell this house about a month or two before the moving date. You need your moving not to be affected by not getting your house sold.

Involve everyone in the family to participate in the completion of this project. Have a regular house meeting. Take ideas from everyone. When your entire family gets involved with the project, it will be less stressful for everyone. Even the kids know that they have an important part to play in this project. Your entire family needs to be on the same page. You can take down ideas from everyone. What are the things they feel should be changed in order to make the house more appealing? You don't need to implement all the ideas right away; you just need to jot down all the ideas. Have a budget for yourself. At the end of the brainstorming meeting, you might have 20 things on your list that need to be done but, with a limited budget, you might not be able to accomplish all of them. Everybody's opinion might be different in regard to priorities, but this is a good time to bring an expert on board, whose job is to sell the property on a regular basis. You know what I mean: a professional realtor.

A true story:

I received a call from Mr. Sherman. He wanted me to come and see his house. They were selling the house because they had bought a bigger house and, in the next few months, they would be moving to the new house. I visited the house and met with his beautiful family. I gave my seller's presentation, and they asked me few more questions on the marketing plan. I came to know that they had recently done some upgrades in the house, which included painting. I noticed that every room in the house had a different colour. As he was showing the property to me, he was telling me about the nice memories attached to the house. In one of the bedrooms, they had a peach/pink colour, which he mentioned was that colour because their elder daughter always wanted it that way. In the next bedroom, I saw a dark blue colour because the boy wanted to have his own space. They spent $3,000 on a fresh coat of paint. I had to remind them that this was not their home anymore. They have to look at it as a project. Different colours were creating divisions, and it made the rooms look much smaller. When it comes to selling a house, I suggest picking neutral colours. Neutral colours give a lot of options and ideas to the potential buyers and make the rooms look much bigger. I also saw some religious pictures in the hallway and in two of the bedrooms. I asked him to remove the religious pictures; the house should give neutral feelings to the potential buyer so that they can start imagining their own personalized items in the home. I suggested that they change the paint and remove the personalized items. At first, they didn't agree because they wanted to save money. We put the house up for sale. There were very few showings scheduled in the first week. At the open house, people provided their feedback that the house was beautiful, but somehow they weren't getting the right vibes. They couldn't explain in words what those vibes were—what was missing or what was too much in the house—but it was not letting them feel the possession of that house. Next week, I was able to convince my seller to get the painting done and take out the personal possessions from the house. With the fresh white paint, and with organizing, the house started looking much bigger. I replaced the old furniture and got the professional staging done. After seeing the well-organized and professionally staged house, my client admitted that it was very difficult for them to accept that it was not their home anymore, and that it was a house that they needed to sell for more. They were confident now. As expected, I sold that house at over asking price and with multiple offers. For privacy reasons, the names have been changed, but you can see their testimonial and many more stories like this on our website at www.VickSahota Homes.com.

So, you have seen, when it comes to selling your house, you need to be practical—you need to listen to your realtor. Your full-service realtor will work with you throughout this entire process.

Constant reminders

Even though you agreed upon the concept of selling your *house* and not your *home*, I will remind you time to time. Every time you think of making a change, think from the prospective of a buyer.

Set a time-line

It is so important for you to understand that time is money. When it comes to selling or buying a house, so many parties are involved. A delay for just a single day can cost you thousands of dollars, so you really need to understand the set time-lines for your project. The day you decide to sell your home, follow these steps:

1. Start looking for a full-service realtor. Interview at least 3.
2. Have a meeting with your family.
3. Create a list of things which need to be done before putting up a *for sale* sign on your lawn.

I'm sure, through this chapter, you will have a clear idea in your mind that, although you are attached to this home, which is not your home anymore, it is a house that you need to sell to get more and more profit out of it. It is a process of complex steps. In order to make it easier for you, I have created a checklist of all the steps involved in this process. You can go to the book website, SellWithVick.com, and download a coloured and print ready format so that you can start working on the checklist right away. Remember: a checklist is a guideline to keep you on the right track. From the checklist, you might choose to do only a few tasks; I must tell you, the more effort you put in, the better the results will be, which means more money.

Sharing my proven techniques

Enjoy a dip in the ocean of our experiences. In this book, you will find a lot of examples, authentic stories, and suggestions and tips for what works and what doesn't work. We are only sharing what worked successfully in selling houses for our clients. But every house is different, and every market is different. Take this book as a guideline to build a customized plan for your house. We are happy to provide you with our suggestions and services; you can contact us at vick@vicksahotahomes.com, or mamta@ viksahotahomes.com.

About the next chapter

With the checklist, you will be overwhelmed with the number of tasks you need to complete to sell the house. You will be surprised, however, how all these jobs can become easier when a professional companion works with you. In the next chapter, I will explain to you how a full service realtor can make your life much easier. You will learn how to select a good realtor who works only for your benefit to get you the desired results. So, don't wait; rush to the next chapter.

ACTION PLAN

_____

_____

_____

_____

_____

_____

_____

_____

_____

_____

_____

_____

_____

_____

_____

_____

_____

_____

_____

_____

_____

_____

_____

_____

_____

Chapter 2

Hire a Realtor
- Vick

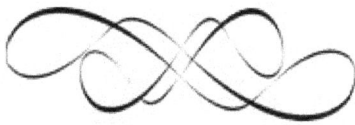

> *"The only source of knowledge is experience."*
> – Albert Einstein

Two choices

Now that you have made up your mind to sell your house, it's time to make a crucial decision. When it comes to selling a house, you have two choices. Number one, you want to put up a house for sale by owner. Number two, you want to hire a professional real estate agent. You often hear advice that it depends on the market. Let's discuss these markets first.

Seller's market: when the number of buyers exceeds the number of homes in the market. When there is less inventory, your house may get sold within a day, and probably with multiple offers, so you might not need a realtor. This is a favorable situation for you, but you're missing the point here. If your property is sold within a day, then that means it is not exposed to many potential buyers.

Even though you have received multiple offers, you have missed a chance to get quality buyers. By saving a few thousand dollars on the realtor's commission, you put yourself at risk of not getting the most out of your property.

Buyer's market: it happens when inventory exceeds the number of buyers. In this market, the best houses are picked up first. In order to sell your home fast, and at a good price, you need to put extra effort and invest some money. Your house will be sold at the top price when it is exposed to many buyers, is marketed well, priced well, and well negotiated to close the deal.

As I discussed with you, selling a home is a project. With the number of steps involved in this project, you don't want to take the responsibility of selling your house on your own and taking on a lot of stress. Don't try to cut corners; it will affect your professional, as well as your personal, life. You will find yourself stuck between doing your regular job or business, taking care of the family and, on the top of everything, showing your house to a number of people. Preparation and presentation of your property needs a professional touch. A small mistake could be very expensive, and you could end up losing high quality, potential buyers.

Hire a professional

For getting a hair-cut, purchasing a business suite, fixing the roof, etc., we hire professionals. Selling a house is a process that you will do only a few times in your lifetime. Do you want to risk the most expensive venture of your life by doing it on your own? Good real estate professionals can provide you with a number of services and get you the highest results in this process. Always remember that a good realtor will always work for the benefit of their clients. When I work with you, my prime objective is to deliver the best services and get the highest price for your property.

Kinds of markets

Although I have already mentioned two of them, there are actually three kinds of markets. Number one is the seller's market, and number two is the buyer's market. Number three is the Equilibrium market (balanced). This topic is so important; I want to explain it in a way that helps you to understand these markets, and to make a decision when it is a good time to sell or buy a property.

Seller's market: in this market, there are less houses available for sale as compared to the number of buyers and, many times, houses sell for over asking price. This is a great time to sell a property.

Buyer's market: in this market, inventory exceeds the supply of buyers, which means there are less buyers in the market. So, unless your property is highly attractive, and exposed in the best way to the potential buyers, it is very difficult to sell your property. Even if you are successful at selling your property, getting a good price will be only possible when you have a strong realtor representing you. A buyer's market is really good for investors; this is the time when they can buy properties at a low price and build their wealth. So, if you're thinking of selling your property in a buyer's market, make sure you have a strong realtor who can work with you through every step of selling your property, from preparation to presentation.

A true story

It was a seller's market; the houses were getting sold within a day. I got a call from Karam. She wanted to sell her property and buy a bigger house, as her parents had moved in with her. Since it was a seller's market, I suggested to secure a property first and then put her house up for sale later. With my strong research and negotiation skills, I was able to secure a beautiful property for her within a week. Now it was time to sell her property at top price.

I put together my staging and marketing team. I started with the declutter consultation. The house was staged with modern furniture and accessories. With quick tips on curb appeal, the house had a million dollar look. I got the drone photography and videography done, as well as the Professional HD photography and Videography done. My team had created fantastic marketing materials such as coloured flyers and booklets, and Facebook and YouTube ads. I set up a date for receiving offers. I hosted a fabulous open house and invited everyone in the neighbor-hood. The open house was advertised heavily over all the social media platforms. I arranged snacks. Three of our team members were there at the open house. I personally talked to everyone who came to the open house and gave a thorough tour of the property. I took their feedback on the property and followed up with everyone. It was a beautifully presented property, so many realtors booked appointments to show the property to their potential buyers. At the day of the offer, I reminded everyone who visited the property. Our hard work paid off—I received multiple offers, not to mention the property was sold for over asking price. My clients were so happy; the next day, Karam called me and mentioned a house that was sold just a week before, in the same neighborhood, at a much lower price. That house owner came to visit her and asked how they had sold their property for much more. She proudly said that her property had sold for more because they had a full service realtor like me. I feel proud to say that my clients are my best brand ambassador. To check out many more testimonials, visit my website at vicksahotahome.com. You will find updated information about the market, and many more tips as well.

A full-service realtor and a discounted one

You must be wondering about the *full-service realtor* term that I have mentioned many times. You might have heard of the term *full-time realtor*. Those were the old days, but sometimes I wonder if realtors are still using the same term. At any rate, a part-time realtor is somebody who has a full-time job and is serving you after that, which ultimately means, you are not his/her priority. A full-time realtor is one who has dedicated himself/herself just for the service of their clients and only dealing in real estate. The next level up from a full-time realtor, is a full-service realtor. A full-service realtor is the professional who takes your house as a project and works with you on each step from preparing the house for sale to presenting the house for maximum exposure. A full-service realtor is a very well connected person in his professional community. Your realtor will work with you and come up with a solid preparation and marketing plan within your budget. There is another term for certain realtors, which is called a discounted realtor. A discounted realtor is the one who will put up a sign on your lawn, maybe take pictures of your property, and will list it on MLS. The discounted realtor might not take much interest in selling the property at a good price. In other words, a discounted realtor might only be interested in selling your property, as compared to a full-service realtor who is interested in selling your property for more. Here are a few things you should expect from your full-service realtor:

1. Property assessment
2. Declutter constitution
3. Staging the house
4. Consultation about the curb appeal
5. Getting the Drone photography and videography
6. Getting HD photography and videography of the house
7. Doing Facebook live, a number of times for the property
8. Promoting the property over various social media platforms
9. Listing your house on various paid and unpaid websites
10. Advertising your property over various radio programs
11. Creating marketing materials such as flyers and booklets
12. Conducting Open Houses
13. Inviting people from the neighborhood and arranging snacks
14. Collecting database and follow-up with potential buyers
15. Receiving offers and strongly negotiating the price of the property
16. Making sure the closing happens smoothly

Now, the decision is yours. Do you want to have a full-service realtor to get you the top price for your property, or are you still looking for a discounted realtor? A full-service realtor might cost you a little more, but keep in mind that a full-service realtor bears a lot of the cost of preparing and presenting your property. A full-service realtor will be advertising your property extensively to get you the best end result, which is more money for your house.

Testimonials link to video on website

I'm sure you're enjoying reading these stories and testimonials. It is more fun to watch the videos. You can go to my website and watch other testimonials, as well as watch my video on the qualities of a full-service realtor: www.SellWithVick.com.

Action plan and about next chapter

Now that you have made the decision to work with a full-service realtor, I must tell you that this is the best decision ever. You will find peace of mind, and have confidence when making the biggest financial decision of your lifetime, which is selling your house.

The next chapter is the most important chapter of this book because it involves a lot of financial commitment. The price of your house will be based on your investment decisions in this step. Without any delay, let's move on to the next chapter to compare small repairs versus a full renovation of your house.

ACTION PLAN

_____

_____

_____

_____

_____

_____

_____

_____

_____

_____

_____

_____

_____

_____

_____

_____

_____

_____

_____

_____

_____

_____

_____

_____

_____

_____

Chapter 3

Small Repairs vs Full Renovation
- Vick

> *"Setting goals is the first step in turning the invisible into the visible."*
> – Tony Robbins

What is your goal?

Now that you have decided to sell your home, and have found a full-service realtor, it is time for the most important decision regarding preparing the house before listing. At this moment, the question arises: should you have renovations done in order to get the highest price for your house? The very first things that may come to your mind will be hardwood flooring, and granite/quartz counter tops in the kitchen and washroom. The cost you're going to invest to have some renovations done, versus the value you will be getting out of it, needs to be assessed. Your realtor will assess the house; based on the assessment, you can work closely with your realtor and create a list of repairs and renovations that need to be done. Based on last year's data and my own experience, I noticed that doing heavy renovations does not get the seller a higher price as compared to small repairs that make the property more movable and appealing.

Cost vs value

Now, it's not the time to go for an entire home renovation, or redo your entire kitchen and bathroom. Buyers are not willing to pay for all those upgrades, but researchers have shown that small fixes and repairs can pay you more value. Replace your garage door, or windows, if required. You might just want to paint them, but it will cost you just a few hundred dollars. I know you love your green paint in your bedroom, but buyers are looking for open space and a place where they can add personal touches, so stick with neutral colours, like white, off-white, or a light gray.

Put on buyers hat

This is the time to put on the buyer's hat and take a walk around your house. You might see a Frisbee on your roof. Just check if there is no shingle missing.

Small repairs you can do that will add huge value to your house are:

1. Fix leaky faucet
2. Fix loose door knobs
3. Replace old fuses or bulbs

4. Replace broken blinds
5. Clean greasy kitchen surfaces
6. Clean the cabinet doors
7. Clean dirty trim or base boards
8. Clean the windows

Consider hiring a handyman

I know you want to save some money and would like to do most of the repairs on your own. Consider hiring a person who can do a better job in less time, and it will be professionally done. By seeing a house, I can tell if the paint was done by a professional or if the homeowner had done it himself. You know I am talking about the edges and trim. These small things can add a lot of value in your property, and vice versa.

Features of *ready to move in* house

A buyer always looks for a *ready to move in* house with an open concept and a place that has a lot of potential to add personal touches.

Here is a list of things a potential buyer would consider to be in a house that is *ready to move in.*

1. Fresh paint
2. No repairs needed
3. All electric fixtures and appliances in working condition

4. Even surfaces
5. Freshly painted garage door and windows
6. No cracks on the driveway
7. Polished hardwood flooring
8. Clean trim and baseboard
9. Fresh and odour free

Get quote for upgrading

After getting the required repairs done and a fresh coat of paint, if you still feel the need to add on some more value, then talk to your realtor. You might feel like adding a granite/quartz counter top in the kitchen, which will add more value to the house. Discuss it with your realtor and get at least three quotes. Select the best quote. Make sure the renovation time is not too long.

Use eco-friendly material

When selecting quotations for materials, always go for eco-friendly ones. Buyers are ready to pay more when they know the materials being used in renovations are eco-friendly. More and more people are cautious and concerned about saving natural resources. So, join the forces and do your part in saving the Earth. I'm sure you'll feel good.

Keep your realtor involved

Although I have mentioned this many times before, I cannot stress the importance enough of involving your realtor in every step—it is crucial. There is a strong reason why I say this. Your realtor is strongly connected with many businesses, and repairing the house is one of their daily tasks. He/she might have really good connections and get the job done at a very good price, which means more and more savings for you. Your realtor will personally follow up with the handyman and any other renovators involved in the process.

Time is the key

Your list might include twenty different things, but keep in mind: *time is the key.* The closing of your new house might be approaching soon; the market can change as well, so stick to your schedule.

Control your emotions

After all those repairs, and a fresh coat of paint, your house will look totally new. You might start getting so many new ideas to decorate this house. At this moment, I have to warn you. Control your emotions. This is not your home anymore; this is the house that you have to sell, and make the most out of it. So, from now on, every addition we make to your house will make it look better and better every time.

Get your complete checklist, and about next chapter

Now that you have a clear idea of what to do, your homework is to make a list of small repairs you need to do, which could get you more value. Also, you need to see if there is any renovation required that could be a must in your potential buyer's list. I know you're very excited and just want to fix that leaking faucet. Meanwhile, you can go to my website, at www.SellWithVick.com, and print a complete checklist of small repair and necessary renovation ideas.

I'm so excited to tell you that, in the next chapter, I will be talking about actually getting more walk-ins to your house. We will be discussing each item that can add value to the exterior of your house, and make your house look more attractive.

ACTION PLAN

_____

_____

_____

_____

_____

_____

_____

_____

_____

_____

_____

_____

_____

_____

_____

_____

_____

_____

_____

_____

_____

_____

Chapter 4

Curb Appeal
- Vick

> *"My belief is you have one chance*
> *to make a first impression."*
> – Kevin McCarthy

Definition and first impression

As per the Merriam Webster dictionary, the definition of *curb appeal* is the visual attractiveness of a house as seen from the street.

According to a famous quotation, *your first impression is your last impression.* When you have a *for sale* sign on your lawn, people who pass by will look at the property. With drone photography, and videography, your property will be shown on various platforms such as MLS, various websites, Facebook, and YouTube. The very first shot is the shot of the community where you live, and the exterior shot of your house.

Key elements

Pay very close attention to the details; it can get you more walk-ins. Curb appeal is the exterior look of the house, and it is the feel of the house. A house should be welcoming enough to attract more potential buyers. It should be so attractive that potential buyers would want to invite their friends and family. After all, having a house is a status symbol. Here is a list of things that you can do to make your curb appeal more attractive.

1. Get rid of any extras in your driveway, e.g., bicycle, water hose, basketball net, or unused car.
2. See if there are any cracks on the driveway. Fill those cracks and have a fresh coat of driveway sealer on it. It will add a lot of value and it won't cost that much.
3. Add a fresh coat of paint on the main door, and the garage door as well.
4. Check those rusty door knobs; treat and polish them.
5. See if the garden bed is in shape. Take out the weeds, and add some mulch; it will restore colour.
6. Check the tiles at the doorstep. If they are uneven, fix them.
7. Add some new flowering plants at the front and in the back yard. It will add a lot of life to your house.
8. Open the curtains and blinds. Curtains that are open look prettier from the street.

9. Add some solar lights to your walkway. Solar lights are economical, and you can place them wherever it will highlight the best attributes of the house.

Get a second opinion

As a homeowner, you might like many things about your house. You just don't notice, or you might just ignore, many defects in the house. Get a fresh set of eyes—talk to your realtor. Your realtor will suggest many good ideas to give a fresh curb appeal. Your own to-do list may be long, but your realtor will suggest what is required the most in order to sell your home fast.

Budget

When you start implementing new ideas to create an attractive curb-appeal, you will start seeing your house going to the next level. You need to be cautious and stick to your budget. Again, I will stress evaluating cost versus value. Do only what is required and suggested by your realtor.

Action plan and what's next

So far, we have spent a few hours in the front yard, and I am sure you are so confident about the curb appeal. Your neighbor might have started asking you if you're selling your house. They will come up with their own ideas to make your house more attractive. Just a word of caution, they will also suggest to you many discounted realtors. They will ask you if their friend can buy the house directly from you. You have come really far in this process to expose your house to most of the potential buyers. Don't settle for less. You can politely suggest that they pass your realtor's information to their friend. People like to talk and like to participate in everybody's business. Just be careful and stick to the plan. In this chapter, your homework is to keep your curb appeal intact. Here is the list of regular tasks:

1. Mow the lawn weekly
2. Pressure wash your driveway and doorstep
3. Take out the weeds
4. Park your car in the garage, not on the driveway; it will hide your exterior.
5. Pick up the trash can and recycling bin as soon as they are emptied.

In the next chapter, I'm going to make your life less stressful. You will be surprised to learn how a small investment can get you a bigger gain. Yes, I will be talking about home inspection.

ACTION PLAN

_____

_____

_____

_____

_____

_____

_____

_____

_____

_____

_____

_____

_____

_____

_____

_____

_____

_____

_____

_____

_____

_____

Chapter 5

Home Inspection
- Vick

> *"A full home inspection ... is the best defense against future liability for the seller and the most assured way a buyer can feel comfortable with the home purchase."*
> – Tony Graham

Usually, a serious buyer would have a formal inspection in the escrow. But with my years of experience, I suggest *you* get the pre-inspection done. There are a lot of benefits associated with it.

Is your home an open book?

Getting a pre-home inspection done shows your willingness to share all the information. It also tells that your house is in good condition. Buyers will be comfortable in considering your house when the home inspection report is attached with marketing materials. This helps a lot in the buyer's market to have an upper hand in the competitive market.

Sell your home faster

Your house would have more chances to sell faster when the home inspection is done prior. You will already know if there is any flaw in the house, and you can get it fixed. A potential buyer will be so confident to put up an offer when they know that the home inspection is done in advance, and the seller doesn't want to hide anything.

Risk of not having a pre-home inspection

When you choose not to have a pre-home inspection, and if the buyer has a condition clause of a home inspection in their offer, and find out about defects in the house, they might ask for a price adjustment— or they might walk away from the deal. It is worth it to spend few hundred dollars to save thousands of dollars in the future.

Your peace of mind

The inspection gives you peace of mind and the confidence for your realtor to negotiate a better deal for you. Talk to your realtor to arrange a pre-inspection for you.

About the next chapter

I know you are now eager to get your house inspected. In the next chapter, I am going to change your life. I will be talking about decluttering. Decluttering can add to your space and make life easier. I can't wait to share ideas about decluttering and organizing with you.

ACTION PLAN

_____

_____

_____

_____

_____

_____

_____

_____

_____

_____

_____

_____

_____

_____

_____

_____

_____

_____

_____

_____

_____

_____

Chapter 6

Declutter
- Mamta

> *"Have nothing in your house that you do not know to be useful, or believe to be beautiful."*
> – William Morris

The pre-home inspection has been done, and you and your realtor are in a much better situation to negotiate a better deal. In this chapter, we are going to talk about decluttering. I know what your first response would be: "I don't have anything in my home to throw away. I use almost everything." I want to remind you that this is not your home anymore; this is the house that you want to sell for more. Talking about selling for more is something very important I want to discuss with you. Whether it is a buyer's market or a seller's market, you cannot control the market. At the same time, you cannot control the location, mortgage rate, or employment rate in your area. Think about what you can change to get more walk-ins.

I know it is very difficult for you to think about decluttering and organizing your house, since you're going to be leaving anyway. Most of my clients who sell their houses, move to bigger houses. You're moving to a new house, so you want to spend most of your time thinking about organizing and starting your life in the new home. It is very difficult for you to put any effort into the one you are still in. Even though you don't want to spend any time decluttering and organizing this house, think from the perspective of your house not being sold because it is too crowded, and then of it staying on the market for much longer. If your house stays on the market for long, it will be an added expense for you. Secondly, if a house stays on the market for long, it may have a negative impact on the listing.

In this chapter, I'm going to share with you how decluttering will sell your house faster, as well as where to start decluttering and how it will be a smooth beginning in your new house.

Benefits of decluttering

Think from a buyer's perspective

The biggest reason most of my clients sell their house is because they're moving to a new house. They're running out of space in this house and now they want to move to a bigger space. In this situation, I can imagine how overcrowded their houses would be. The clothing cabinets will be full. There will be more furniture as compared to the space in the house. If your house is on the market in the same situation, it will turn off potential buyers. Your reason to move out from this house should not become the reason for potential buyers not to purchase your house. Your house may be an ideal house for the potential buyer but, if they cannot see it properly, or feel it, you don't have a sale. The simple act of decluttering can make a huge difference.

You will emotionally move out

As I discussed at the very beginning of this chapter, this is not your home anymore; when you start decluttering, you will feel that you are emotionally moving out of your house. You will start thinking like a business person who wants to sell a house, and sell a house for more.

Planning ahead

Decluttering for the purpose of selling your house means that you are packing everything that is not going to help you with the sale of the house and is not a necessity at this moment. By starting to pack ahead of time, you will be all set for the move to your new house.

New home, new beginning

I know you're excited about moving to your new home, and I'm sure you don't want to start your life in a new house with the old clutter. New home, new beginning! You really want to keep your new home as beautiful as it is. You don't want to make the same mistakes that you have made in your old house. I'm sure that you will only want to keep those things that you would like to take to the new home. So, this process of decluttering will help you to sort it out.

Focus on what your buyer wants

Meanwhile, put on your buyer's hat and visualise what a potential buyer would like to see in their dream house. Just by starting to think and act in this manner will help you to have your house on the buyer's *favorite* list.

Maximizing space by minimizing things

Did you notice, just by removing that old rug from the living room, your living room opens up? You will fall in love with the hardwood flooring. I know you've thrown a lot of house parties, and the three-piece sofa worked great throughout the years. But it does not align with the dimensions of your living room. You might just want to keep a loveseat and an armchair. This will open up your space; buyers can see and imagine their own personal space when the room looks more spacious.

3-step process

I know you're totally sold on the idea of decluttering your house to get more value for your house—but you don't know where to start. There are three steps involved in this process:

1. Identifying the genuine clutter

Look for the things that you have not used for a year. It could be your old rug that you have kept in one of the closets when you bought the new one. It could be the old bicycle that your kids are not using anymore. Genuine clutter could be your old desktop computer, which is not serving any purpose but is still holding space at your desk. Women, especially, keep their old clothing in a hope that one day they will get back in shape. I just want to remind them that trends change every year, so they need to be careful; nobody wants to look outdated. I personally prefer to donate clothing if I have not worn it for more than a year. Believe me, if you have not worn something for a year, you will never wear it again. Clutter not only takes up space in our house; it also takes up space in our mind. Remember, your clutter could be a useful item for somebody; so, sell it, donate it, or do whatever you want to do, but do not keep the clutter in your house.

2. Items that are not helpful in selling your house

Once you get rid of all the items that you had not used over the years, you will start seeing more space in your house. Do not stop here! Now it's time to wear a buyer's hat. Look for unnecessary items that are taking up space on the floor, on the walls, and in the cabinets. Instead of having eight chairs at your dining table, you might want to go with six chairs. Look at the cabinets. If they're full of bedding or towels, it will give a feeling of suffocation. Just keep what is necessary; it should look spacious.

Look for space that is not utilized properly. For example, you might like creating music, so you have turned one of the bedrooms into your music studio. Pack all the unnecessary items and turn it into a bedroom.

The third important step is to now become a photographer. Take pictures of all of your rooms. Don't worry; I am not going to use these pictures for promotions. Look at these pictures from the perspective of a buyer. You might find, in some rooms, that the furniture looks too big as compared to the layout of the room. You might see that the kitchen shelf looks smaller in the pictures. Look at it from a buyer's perspective, and then think of how you can make the space bigger. You might want to move some furniture around. For example, the headboard of your bed is adjacent to the window. You did it for your convenience and for more or less lighting. But your bedroom is rectangular. This setting does not go with the layout; you need to change it. I know it is difficult; you might not sleep for one or two nights, but you will get used to it. You need to remind yourself that you're working towards selling this house to a potential buyer.

Here is an important question, which I often get asked: Where are we going to put the excessive furniture and items, since we're not moving right now? You have two options: number one, you can rent a storage space and keep all the items there. Remember, you're not going to keep the items that you will not be using in the future. Number two, you can ask your friends or family to keep this extra stuff in their garage. This is my least favorite option because your items are valuable and you should not keep them anywhere out of your control.

I know you will feel a little uncomfortable living with minimalism, but you have to understand that the situation is temporary. You will move to your new house soon, and you will have all the freedom to live the way you want.

Key points

I find this chapter very important, not only from the point of view of selling a house, but because it's the first step toward living a peaceful and serene life. I'm going to jot down key points that we have discussed in this chapter. Make sure you're taking notes. You can also go to my website at www.SellWithVick.com, and download a coloured, full page, print ready checklist to start working right away. So, here are the key points we have discussed so far:

1. Get rid of genuine clutter
2. Maximize space by minimizing furniture
3. Live with minimalism; it's a temporary state
4. Utilize every room
5. Keep it intact

I know decluttering sounds like a huge investment of time, but I promise that it will increase the value of your house. The time that you invest in decluttering and organizing will save you time in the new house.

I can't tell you how excited I am about the upcoming chapter; it's my favorite topic. Being a colour analyst, I love working with colourful themes. Colours simply add life to a *dead* room. It is the most important step in this entire sales and marketing process. So, the next chapter is *Staging Your House.*

ACTION PLAN

_____
_____
_____
_____
_____
_____
_____
_____
_____
_____
_____
_____
_____
_____
_____
_____
_____
_____
_____
_____
_____
_____
_____
_____
_____

Chapter 7

A Five Star Hotel Look
- Mamta

> *"Home staging is no longer optional in the real estate market; it is a must!"*
> – Barbara Corcoran

Remember your last visit to a luxury hotel, where everything looked so clean? I just love seeing those clean bed sheets, and fresh flowers on the side table, which add a lot of life and depth to the room. I feel so pampered trying those chocolates wrapped just for me. I get excited about the neatly stacked towels. That's the best experience. You know why we like these hotels—because of the cleanliness and those special touches and attention to detail.

When buyers are looking for a home, they are looking for a place that is welcoming. A buyer gets so excited by coloured themes and systematically organized furniture. I am talking about staging. But you will say that your house is really neat and clean; so, why would you need to do staging? I know you like the ethnic cushions and your special rug that came from Italy, but you need to understand that our objective is to make your place spacious and attractive—only let stay what fits into this category.

You can do the home staging on your own. If you have a full-service realtor, talk to him/her. Your realtor should have a stager who can work with you, within your budget, to make your house welcoming and attractive. When it comes to staging, don't try to save money; a professionally staged house can get you more money than one that isn't. Here are a few benefits of having home staging:

More walk-ins

Your house is competing against hundreds of other houses on MLS. The only chance your house has to get picked out is when the pictures of your house are attractive enough.

Time is money

Everyone is busy, so how does a potential buyer know that you have a beautiful house to sell? First, your house needs to be sold visually, which means the buyer's realtor needs to love the house, and be convinced enough to send the listing to his/her client. If a realtor is sending ten good listings to the potential buyer, because of a lack of time, the buyer does not look for an ideal house at the beginning. They do the elimination round. How it works is, the buyer will go through listings quickly and just start eliminating those that do not fit into his/her criteria. When your house is beautifully staged, it has more chances to be picked out for showing.

Sell for more

Most buyers buy a house emotionally. When they enter the house, if they love the entrance and like the spread of colours throughout the living room, they fall in love with the house. As I have said, "A first impression is the last impression." If the first impression is good, a buyer will look for more selling features. When the first impression is bad, a buyer starts the elimination process. Sometimes the buyer can't express in words what is actually working, but it is the ambience that you have created by the beautiful placement of furniture and accessories. When a buyer loves the house, he/she is even ready to pay more because it is not a temporary arrangement. It is a long term commitment, so there are no compromises.

Your house sells faster

Whether it is a seller's market or a buyer's market, good houses get picked up first. With staging, you will get more walk-ins to your house. With more walk-ins, you will have more chances to get it sold faster, and for a higher selling price.

Emotional buying

As I have discussed before, although buyers want to stay practical, most of the time they're emotionally sold. When the house looks beautiful, the ambience is calm and soothing, and the layout is spacious, buyers will just ignore or might not notice some flaws in the house; your house has more chances to sell faster at a good price, even in the competitive market.

Are you living in the house, or is it vacant?

Because this topic is so important, it can make or break the deal. I will discuss each room in detail with you. In this chapter, you will learn how to stage your house. You will get tips on how to highlight key features and downplay some flaws. Whether you are living in the house at present, or the house is vacant, staging is a must.

Sometimes clients say, "The house is vacant, so why do I need to put furniture in it? People can see it is spacious and would like to put in an offer." I would like to remind you that this is old school. In this competitive market, buyers want to see a potential space—not a building. So, it doesn't matter whether you're living in the house still full of furniture; if the house is vacant, you should stage it.

How to stage a house:

Deep cleaning the house

With decluttering, the house has already started looking spacious; it's time to take the next step: deep cleaning. I suggest you hire professional cleaners to get the deep cleaning done. I know you have stainless steel appliances. They look great, but how about those sticky fingers? The tiles look great, but how about the grout? You need to get everything deep cleaned; remember that five star hotel look. Deep cleaning will cost you a few hundred dollars, but it will make your house sparkling clean and get you the best selling price.

Get the painting done

I know that you love personalized touches, but have a neutral paint colour throughout your house. Neutral coloured paint makes a space look bigger. Also, neutral colours gives the buyer a chance to wear his/her creative hat and imagine various options. Let's say that you have a small kitchen. You should have one neutral color in the kitchen and eat-in area. It will make the entire space look much bigger.

Make use of awkward spaces

Staging is not just decoration; its main objective is to showcase that the place has a lot of potential. For example, sometimes all rooms are not completely rectangular or square; there are some extra corners or spaces. Think of adding a fish tank in that area. You might want to use a small table, and add some books and a laptop. Give it the look of your own personalized office space. Remember the importance of having proper lighting as well, so add some light to highlight that corner.

Adding pot lights

I understand how you might like yellow light bulbs in your bedroom and other areas because it adds calmness. But, remember, we talked about the hotel look; we need complete lighting so that the room looks bigger. You must replace your yellow light bulbs with white light bulbs. Also, consider adding pot lights when it comes to selling your house. Pot lights are an inexpensive way to add extra light in a house. Recently, when preparing a house for sale, I suggested to my clients that they get pot lights installed on the main floor. They liked my idea. I arranged it with my team and got the pot lights put in. My clients called me that same evening, and said, "Oh, my God, we lived in this house for 11 years, and now we realize that we lived in the dark all those years."

Smell in the house

For some reason, I don't go to Chinese restaurants to eat. I can't bear the smell of their spices, but I love Chinese food. So, I go to other restaurants that serve a mix of international foods. You might not notice the smell of your spices or the oils but, when some outsiders enter, they notice the odour. Our objective should be to give a nice fresh feeling to the potential buyers. Nothing should distract them. Although every potential buyer enters a house with the hope that this house could be his/her dream house, always remember that they will always look for reasons to eliminate the house. It's just natural; this is the biggest investment of their lifetime, and he/she doesn't want to make any mistakes. So, while your house is for sale, make sure you do not use strong spices. If required, add room freshener, but not one that is too strong.

Staging every corner of your house:

Living room

1. Have less furniture in the living room; it should be welcoming. When you have a separate living and family room, you should keep the living room for guests and hosting parties. So, make it fun, make it exciting, and make it happen.
2. A common myth is to have furniture pushed against the wall to make it look bigger, but this isn't the case. In fact,

move your furniture around. Group your furniture in a way that it will be a smooth flowing room.

3. Use contemporary furniture in the living room. The living room is a place where you invite your friends and your family. You give them a chance to come and enjoy your open space and lifestyle. The contemporary furniture adds a lot of fun. When you have neutral colours on the walls, and have contemporary furniture, your living room looks exquisite.

4. Now, it's time to accessorize the living room. You can add a few cushions and a neutral coloured rug. Pick up one accessory and design the entire theme around it. When it comes to adding colours, I always go with the odd number.

5. Let's say your theme colour is turquoise green. You can start with one statement piece, which could be a nice turquoise green coloured cushion, and then you could add a few more cushions. Pick a white base with a touch of turquoise green. Accessories on the side and center table can have off-white and rusty gold colours. Instead of having decoration pieces in a row, go with a triangle shape. Depending on the layout of the room, you can add paintings and wall hangings. When it comes to staging, I believe *less is more.* I only add a few key pieces, which can keep my buyers interested in the room.

Bedroom

1. If your house is a four-bedroom, make sure you are staging all four bedrooms.
2. Making one room as a home office will distract potential buyers. If you're using any room as a home office, or as a recreation room, pack your stuff. Remember, it is just a temporary phase. Buy a bed frame and an air mattress, and dress up the bed.
3. I strongly suggest hiring a professional stager to stage the house from top to bottom. It seems like an expensive investment, but this investment is worthwhile.
4. Open the curtains in all the bedrooms.
5. If you have a standing steamer, give finishing touches to your bed.
6. Have lots and lots of pillows and cushions on the bed.
7. A throw will work magic.
7. I strongly recommend not using a bedding set; the quilt will make your room look smaller.
8. Put a contemporary lamp on the side table.
9. Add a few key pieces and wall paintings.
10. Colours always play a prime role when it comes to liking or disliking a room in an instant.
11. Clean and organize walk-in closets.
12. My favorite store is HomeSense. The moment I enter the store, my vague ideas just start taking shape. I can find anything in this store. I would definitely say it is a one stop shop.

13. You can check out my book website, www.sellwith vick.com, to find more creative ideas, and many before and after pictures of home staging.

Washroom

1. The washroom is a place where a person goes, not only for cleaning purposes, but for their own quiet time. So, think big; think of a luxury spa.
2. Make sure the counter tops are clean.
3. You can also add some fresh flowers.
4. If you think buyers won't open the cabinets, you are wrong. Clean and organize the cabinets.
5. Hang towels neatly; there are lot of videos on YouTube that can teach you how to fold towels.
6. The toilet needs to be extra clean, and working properly.
7. Remove your medication and personal items.
8. Add mats in the washroom.
9. Put up a new shower curtain.
10. Add final touches with scented candles.
11. Make sure the mats, shower curtain, and candles in the washroom all go with a colour theme.

Kitchen and dining area

1. The countertops need to be sparkling clean.
2. Remove almost everything from the counters.
3. Put some fruit in a basket. It will add colour to your counter.

4. The dishwasher needs to be clean and stain-free.
5. Organize all the cabinets.
6. Make sure there are no dirty dishes in the sink.
7. Add a table runner.
8. Place fancy plates and cutlery on the dining table. Make sure it is not crowded.
9. Remove sticky notes from the outside of the fridge, and clean and organize the inside.

Things to consider

1. Make sure not to leave any expensive jewellery out in the open.
2. Don't have any stickers on the doors.
3. Remove unnecessary electronic items.
4. Make sure doors are opening and closing smoothly.
5. All bulbs should be working properly.
6. Make sure there is natural light in all the rooms.
7. Pay attention to details.
8. Add colours, but make sure there are not too many colours in each room.
9. Go with contemporary furniture only.

Preparation to presentation

Now that your house is fully prepared, it is time to take the next step in this process. In the next chapter, you will learn how you are going to get rewarded for your hard work. You will learn how to present your house in order to sell it for more.

ACTION PLAN

_____
_____
_____
_____
_____
_____
_____
_____
_____
_____
_____
_____
_____
_____
_____
_____
_____
_____
_____
_____
_____
_____
_____
_____

Chapter 8

Go Where Your Clients Are
- Mamta

> *"To catch mice, put bait where they often travel.*
> *Same idea for finding clients."*
> – Roger Ellerton

How do you receive information?

If you're like me, you are checking updates on Twitter at least twice a day. Do you like to check your favourite movie stars' Facebook pages? You might want to check out the latest videos from your favourite YouTubers. Do you check your emails first thing in the morning? Or do you go to your favourite news site and scroll through the current news?

Did you notice that I was talking about online media? I'm not saying that you don't ever pick up a hard copy of the newspaper, but you might only do it once in a week. Every person is holding a smartphone; it is much easier to access any information online. In this fast moving world, it is very hard to find the time to read the details of every news article, so we just glance through the headlines. The fastest way to stay connected and updated with information is through Twitter, YouTube, and email. Your phone keeps you updated and sends notifications about what is happening around you. Things have changed a lot in the last decade. When you think of attracting buyers, think from the perspective of the easiest, fastest, and most frequent ways to reach your potential buyers.

How often do you check your facebook?

These days, we eat, sleep, dance ... with Facebook. Facebook has more than 2 billion subscribers, which is higher than the most populated country in the world. The Facebook population is even bigger than the combined population of China and India. Remember, as I told you before, to hire a realtor who has a strong social media presence. With a strong social media presence, your realtor can promote you through various platforms over social media. My personal favourite is Instagram. I just love seeing beautiful pictures and can spend hours looking at the beautiful destinations. Mostly, people like to see what others are doing on Facebook. They enjoy seeing how others are living their lives. Many people check their Facebook at least 10 times a day. What are you thinking? Do you want to have your property advertised only on MLS? No way! Potential buyers need to see your property first thing in the morning with their breakfast. They need to enjoy looking at the staging while they are having their lunch. By evening, they should like, comment, and even share your property with someone in their circle. Strange, isn't it? But it is true. People naturally like to share good stuff. When your property is beautifully staged and professionally photographed, people will love to share it. They feel pride in sharing something that is worth sharing.

How online media works

1. Your realtor should post one new video every day till the property is sold. It seems like a lot of work. Professional realtors know the importance of social media. When potential home buyers see the property, the first thing they will do is call their realtor to view that property. Their realtor becomes obligated to show them the property. A second scenario would be that a potential buyer will call their realtor to book a showing. In that case, your realtor is in a strong position to highlight all the fabulous features of the house.

2. In regard to videos, every video needs to be unique and fabulous. People need to get the feeling that they are actually visiting your house. It has to be tempting enough to have hundreds of showings in the very first week. What do you think the result would be? When someone books a showing based on high quality photos, videos, and presentation, they are already sold on the property. They just want to touch it, feel the vibes, and see if the property is welcoming enough to bring their friends and family over. Buyers see the

beautifully staged property and, when they get the feature sheet in their hand, they get the feeling of possession. With a staged house, they start getting tons of ideas, such as how they are going to organize and decorate their house.

3. Getting back to social media, most clients like to put in an offer after the first, or at maximum, the second visit. They may want to take some time and ask their realtor to show them some more properties. Again, the new video of your property will be seen on Facebook, Twitter, and Instagram, and even as a motivation video or music video on YouTube. Your ad will be everywhere! The motive is to occupy the potential client's mind so that they only see your property. They need to start feeling connected with your property. Let's explain this phenomenon with an example. You are planning to buy a Honda Accord this year. You are looking at finances, checking with the insurance company, and thinking about selling your existing car. Guess what? On the road, wherever you go, you now see Honda Accords. You see them when you are at a traffic light; you see them at your kids' school; and you even see them when you are in the parking lot. Most of the parking lot is full of Honda cars. In the evening, you turn on the TV to watch your favourite show. What the hell—again, Honda. How is it possible? The truth is, your mind only started noticing Hondas the moment you decided to buy one. It is the same way when your property is advertised throughout every social media platform; your

potential buyer's mind will notice that property again and again.

4. Now, have you started to feel the power of social media, and understand the importance of hiring a full-service realtor who can give your property this much exposure? I strongly suggest working very closely with your realtor to create the entire social media strategy. You lived in this house for years. No one knows this property better than you. You are the one who has experienced the property in all the seasons, and you are the only one able to speak from your heart about this property.

5. Sit with the marketing team of your realtor, and aggressively participate in every process. If possible, record a video about your experience living in the house, and how you are looking for a deserving buyer who can take care of the property, just like you did.

Do you and your kids watch TV or YouTube?

Here is an interesting observation: kids now like to watch YouTube videos instead of TV programs. They would like to know more about what's happening in the life of their favourite YouTuber, instead of any animated movies on TV. Speaking of movies, it is much easier for kids to access movies through Netflix or YouTube. So, think from the perspective of a buyer; if you're watching your favorite motivational speaker, and you see an ad for a beautifully staged house in your city, what will be your first response? You will pick up your phone and, without wasting a moment, you will call the realtor whose number is highlighted on the screen, to book an appointment. You can send the link for this property to your friend because your friend is looking for a house in the same neighborhood.

What attracts you?

What kind of information attracts you? You might be interested in seeing new trends in the fashion industry. Do you like to see what's happening in politics? Or you might just be interested in the local news. Just like you, your potential buyers come from various walks of life. Your online marketing team will reach your potential buyer through different platforms, and keep the interaction going. A social media specialist's job is to understand the buyer's psychology and demographic, and then prepare a great marketing plan to attract those buyers.

A final thought

Now that we have discussed the importance of online media, I'm sure you must have started paying more attention to all sorts of ads you are receiving through various platforms. When you think about promoting your property online, the very first thing is to talk to your full-service realtor, who has a very strong online hold. A good realtor always welcomes your suggestions and would like to involve you in each and every step of presenting your property to potential buyers. I know, at this stage, you're so curious to know how to market your property. In the next chapter, I will be working on various marketing materials and how to prepare and present those materials in the market. I can't wait to share this information with you!

ACTION PLAN

Chapter 9

Complete Marketing Plan & Implementation
- Mamta

> *"The man who stops advertising to save money is like the man who stops the clock to save time."*
> – Henry Ford

Listing your house

The job of the resumé is to get you an interview, not the job. During the interview, you sell your skills and, ultimately, get the job. Similarly, the objective of listing a house is to get more potential buyers to step inside your house.

There are two key elements of getting more walk-ins. First, you need attractive photos, audio, and video presentation. I have already discussed the importance of professional photography and videography. In this chapter, I will discuss in detail what kind of marketing materials need to be created.

Second, is the listing price. Let's discuss *listing price* in detail.

Listing price

Pricing your house is a very crucial step in this process. Market conditions will heavily affect the pricing of your property. Depending on the area, similar properties in the neighbourhood, recent comparable sales, etc., a professional realtor can strategically price your property. When I work with my clients, I keep my clients in the loop. I prepare an entire marketing plan, pricing strategy, and customized design for their house.

Marketing materials

Whether you own a small condo or a huge five-bedroom house, marketing should not be compromised in any case. I strongly believe in creating a good mix of traditional and contemporary marketing materials. Here is a list of some key marketing materials, which can help you sell your house faster, and add an additional 5% onto the selling price of your house (If you have a full- service realtor, you just need to stay connected and enjoy the entire marketing process.):

Professional HD photography

With DSLR cameras and high pixel mobiles, anyone can take pictures of your house. But to get the right angle, proper lighting, and professional editing, a professional real estate photographer needs to do it for you. When pictures are not appealing, we miss a lot of opportunities. Everyone is busy. Due to their time restrictions, when being sent a list of properties by a realtor, the buyers usually want to see the properties that appeal to their eyes the most. I never compromise on standards. I get professional photography done for my clients at my cost.

HD virtual tour

Seeing pictures is one thing, but when you see a virtual tour of the house, you get excited. Nice music, and zoom-in and zoom-out pictures, creates a kind of riddle. Humans love riddles and want to solve them. So, an HD Virtual tour is the next step to professional photography. You can check my website, vicksahotahomes.com, to see examples of virtual tours for my clients.

Feature sheet

Buyers usually see a number of houses before they decide which one they want to put an offer on. Prepare promotional packages of your property and hand them out. The feeling of possession is like holding the key to the house. My professional designers create attractive and informative feature sheets of your property; buyers not only experience the house but they get a lot of information about the neighbourhood.

Drone photography

The next step to HD Photography is Drone Photography. It gives an idea of what the neighbourhood is like. Your potential buyer will be so excited seeing photos taken by drone, and would be more motivated to pick your neighbourhood.

Drone videography

Next to photos, videos are my favourite. It seems like a complete communication. Your potential buyer gets to see the traffic flow on your street. Drone videos are so successful nowadays.

Your own house website

Trust me! Your house needs to have its own website. All online advertisement will direct the potential buyer to your website. When a buyer is redirected to your website, then you have full control to showcase him/her the key features of the house. You can also lead a buyer to a desired action; for example, call now or book an appointment. Isn't it neat! All marketing efforts lead towards your website. This way you will never lose a potential buyer.

Tip: I am even taking it one step further. With retargeting, even if your potential buyers leave your site, they will see your ad whenever they open any google partner website. Talk to your realtor about this cool feature.

Ads on various websites

Various buyers look for houses on websites other than www.realtor.ca. There are a number of websites based on the area in which you live; for example: kijiji.ca; craigslist.ca; homefinder.ca; etc.

Talk to your realtor and make sure your house is listed on all the relevant websites. Your realtor will need to invest some money to get your house advertised on some of the websites.

Radio ads

While driving to work or picking up kids from school, you like to listen to the radio. What better place to have your house advertised than on the radio? I must say this is a straight *call to action* platform. A potential buyer will call your realtor right away. Make sure your realtor has a strong presence on various radio frequencies. Also, make sure that your realtor can advertise your ad a number of times from morning to evening.

Newspaper

An aggressive buyer looks at all media for their dream home. Never leave out a newspaper in your marketing campaign. Please make sure that your realtor has a marketing consultant who can pick catchy words to attract more buyers.

Flyers and door hangers

Work with a good creative artist to prepare an attractive flyer for your house. If you are living in an area where people speak various languages, get your flyer translated into at least five dominating languages. You should be aggressive and get door hangers made.

Online ads

90 percent of home buyers searched online at some point during their home buying process. My marketing team specializes in placing social media ads on various platforms such as Facebook, Instagram, YouTube, and Google. With globalization, you can also expect to attract buyers from distant regions, or international investors. Online advertisement takes our message globally.

Facebook ads

Facebook ads are a very effective way of promoting your house, as well as the least expensive way. If your realtor has a strong followership, many potential buyers will be checking his/her updates on social media. Every time your realtor goes live to talk about your property, all of his friends and followers get notified. You can run multiple ads to highlight key features of the house at the same time.

YouTube ads

Anyone who is searching for a desired property will land on your YouTube ad when it is professionally created and placed. Prepare a video tour of your house: in today's online world, videos are seen 20 times more, as compared to texts or pictures. If you are selling your home on your own, take a camera and shoot a video of your entire home; post it every day with editing on various social media platforms. When I work with my clients, my marketing team creates virtual tours, drone photography and videography, open house invites, and house tour videos, all for you at my cost.

Email marketing

A successful realtor must have a large database. As soon as your property is listed, your realtor will start sending emails to his/her database of potential buyers.

Even though all social media platforms are great, I cannot deny the importance of direct email. When a potential buyer sees a property in his/her drop box, he/she will definitely open it. With the advanced media, your realtor can check how many times the potential buyer has actually opened the email and seen the property. Someone who has watched the video more than once is a serious buyer. Your focus should be on serious buyers.

Quality vs Quantity

When it comes to creating a budget for marketing materials, I get this question often: should we go for quality material and have fewer materials, or should we go for a number of materials and constant ads? My answer to this question is always to have a good balance. Now, at this moment, you will be scratching your head and saying, "Oh, what an average answer." Let me explain to you in detail how you can achieve a desired result with balance. You need to learn what materials need more attention to detail and what materials need to be casually presented. Creating key marketing material, like photos and videos, I go with quality work because that is the base of all the offline and online marketing materials. When it comes to posting regularly on Facebook and YouTube ads, I go with the quantity; the number of times you're knocking on the door of your potential buyers on those platforms, matter. Every time your potential buyer is seeing the ad, it needs to look unique. On my book website, www.sellwithvick.com, you will find a number of marketing materials. You will also find samples of flyers and door hangers.

About the next chapter

Now that you have started your marketing campaign, you will be flooded with calls coming from all marketing sources. People who are driving by your property will see your *house for sale* sign, and will be calling your realtor; your realtor will be booking the showings. You will be booked with back-to-back showings. You must be getting really excited about it. Wow! It's a good response; your hard work has started to pay off. On Facebook, you will see that people have started asking the price of the property. So, finally, this is working. Hold your excitement! Now, your responsibility is going to increase. In the next chapter, Vick is going to share how the biggest challenge has just started. But if you are cautious, and follow the steps, you are very close to making a sale.

ACTION PLAN

Chapter 10

Open Your Doors and Close The Deal
- Vick

> *"Only one thing counts in this world: get them to sign on the line which is dotted."*
> – Alec Baldwin, as Blake, in *Glengarry Glen Ross*

Congratulations! You are getting flooded with phone calls. Your calendar is full of back-to-back showings. Let's take a moment to go through each step before having your first showing. I believe this is the most important chapter of this book because, so far, whatever you were doing, it was only you, and me, your realtor, but now it's show-time. Many potential buyers will be coming to your house with the hope that they can find their dream house, and make a life there. So, this is a very delicate situation; you need to be very cautious because even a slight move can make or break a deal. Don't be afraid; I am with you every step of the way. I will walk you through the entire process. Also, you can go to the book website, www.SellWithVick.com, and download the to-do check-list of Opening Your Doors for Potential Buyers.

Requests for showing To-Do list

When your house is listed, and you start booking appointments for showings, here is a list of things you should do every day to keep your place intact:

1. Your beds need to be made every morning by 9:00 a.m.
2. The washroom needs to be sparkling clean and dry.
3. The washroom counter tops need to be clean.
4. If you're using any supplies, put them back in the vanity cabinets.
5. Keep the place looking the same as when you finished staging.
6. Try cooking in the morning for the entire day.
7. Keep the kitchen counter tops clean and empty.
8. Open the windows so that food smells or any other kinds of odours can go away. Burn scented candles when you are at home.
9. Make sure there are no excess towels or extra clothes lying on the floor, even in the laundry room. Put everything in their baskets, neatly stacked.
10. Make sure you leave the home before every showing. If you're in the house, it means the house is already occupied. How can a potential buyer think of fitting into your space? Let the buyer explore your house. A buyer would like to feel the possession of the space. A potential buyer would like to talk about furniture arrangement, traffic flow, and me-time options. When a realtor shows the house, the prime objective is match-

making. Buying a house is a long-term commitment. A realtor has a list of *must-haves* for his/her buyers. While showing, the realtor will put emphasis on the key features of the house, and will also share if there are any minor or major concerns. Buyers will openly ask a number of questions and also ask for suggestions. It is their opportunity to explore the house, inside and outside, before they make a decision to put in an offer. Make sure you give them this chance to open their heart and fall in love with your house.

Open house

An open house is a little different than a showing. With a showing, a realtor gives a personal tour of the house, and the potential buyer spends half an hour to an hour in the house. The buyer explores the house, inside and out, and discusses the features and concerns openly. A potential buyer will find they are more comfortable with a private showing, and it is easier for them to make a decision. An Open house is different; in an open house, you open up doors for potential buyers, and people come to see the house. Compared to a private showing, their visit is short at an open house. From the buyer's perspective, they need to visit 10 other houses that fit into their criteria, in the next 2 hours. From the realtor's perspective, so many buyers are visiting at the same time; so, even if there are many people on the realtor's team to assist the buyers, it is still impossible to give a personal tour to the potential buyer. In this amount of time, chances are low of getting the feel of the house and falling in love with it. You need to plan an open house in a way that a potential buyer will stay a little bit longer and build a rapport with your realtor. This gives your realtor more time to sell the key features of the house. Here are a few key points you need to follow at the open house:

1. Open house signs should be placed throughout the neighborhood, first thing in the morning.
2. Open house times need to be specified on the *house for sale* sign, as well as on MLS and realtor.ca to generate more footfall.
3. Arrange some snacks (finger foods are easier to eat and create less mess) so that they spend more time in your house and feel welcomed.
4. Make sure your realtor is taking everybody's information. When your realtor follows up with potential buyers, he/she can book a showing for the interested parties.
5. Make sure all the marketing materials are in place, and everybody gets a copy of a feature sheet booklet. A potential buyer may visit many open houses on the same day. A buyer will lost track of your house. When you hand out the feature sheet to the buyer, there are more chances for the buyer to remember your house.
6. Many people come to an open house, and it could get a little messy. Your job is to clean the house as soon as the open house is completed; you never know when

you will receive a call to book your next showing. Being proactive is the key to selling your home faster and for a record breaking price.

When to do an open house

Now, I am going to share a success secret with you. You might have only heard about having open houses over the weekend, but have you thought of conducting an open house during a weekday? I, personally, like to do an open house at least once on a weekday, after school hours or in the evening. Imagine when parents are walking their kids home from school, or coming back from work on a Friday evening, and they see your *Open House* sign that says to explore the house and enjoy fresh lemonade. That will bring serious buyers: someone who rents an apartment and would like to purchase a house in the same neighbourhood; someone owns a home in the area and wants their friend or family member to move to their neighbourhood. Add this plan in your wish list, and discuss this option with your realtor.

Receiving offers and negotiations

WOW, you have received an offer; that's wonderful! It's a good beginning. Don't panic if the offer is too low; trust your realtor. Don't be in a rush to say no to the offer. Always keep the conversation going. Your realtor will discuss this strategy in detail with you. This is the time when you need to be patient and let the realtor do his job. Stick to your daily to-do list till the time you close the deal. Sometimes it takes a little bit longer, depending on whether you are in a buyer's market or in a seller's market. Stick to the plan, promote your property regularly, and keep it presentable—you will have more chances of closing the deal faster and at your desired price.

Congratulations! Your house is sold!

So, the hard work has finally paid off. You have received a great offer and made the sale. It is time for the party.

You have been really patient and, by this time, you might have started liking your 5-star hotel looking house, and you just feel like keeping it intact. Well, I'm serious about this: you will need to keep your house intact. Your closing may be in the next few days or the next few weeks. So, till the closing, you have to keep this house in the same shape in which the buyers agreed to buy it. In my experience, I have seen houses get sold at once; but, in some situations, the contracts get terminated, or the sellers get paid less because they didn't keep the house in good shape. This is not your house anymore; you are just acting as a caretaker of the house. Your responsibility has increased now. The buyer is expecting to get the house in the same shape as when he/she put an offer on it. Here is a checklist of things you need to keep in mind and follow till closing:

1. Mow the lawn weekly.
2. Keep the house clean.
3. Make sure there are no new scratches on the walls or on the floors.
4. Make sure there are no new stains on the carpet.

Buyer revisit

After the offer has been accepted, and before the day of closing, the buyer will schedule one or two visits, based on your agreement. Please be extra cautious to keep the house neat and clean. At any point, the buyer should not regret their purchase.

Live with minimalism

Make sure you do not bring back boxes from storage. Keep on living with minimalism till your closing. It is very easy to fall back in the old habits. Always keep in mind that you are now only a caretaker of this house.

Closing checklist

Here is a checklist you need to follow before and on the day of closing:

1. Get your address changed.
2. Make arrangements with the moving company.
3. Talk to your internet service provider about your move

and receive uninterrupted services.

4. If you have kids, inform the school and get the address changed.
5. Make sure you have arranged how you will be commuting from the new house to your workplace.
6. The day of the closing will be overwhelming. Make sure you arrange for food in advance. You don't want to pack and unpack utensils. Order food from outside. When I work with my clients, I arrange their entire day's meals so that they can just focus on a smooth move.
7. Sweep and mop the floors once all the furniture has been moved. You should leave the house clean for the buyer.
8. Make sure you move everything. Never ask to keep any furniture in the garage; the new homeowner wants to have the feeling of possessing the entire house, so don't spoil their fun. It's a time of new beginning for you as well.
9. You have to leave all extra keys, garage door remotes, and any instructions and/or manuals, on the kitchen counter.

A new beginning

By going through the step-by-step process of selling your house, I'm sure, by now, you have emotionally moved out from your old home and are looking forward to enjoying your time in your new home. I would be happy to hear about your selling experience, and I would be more than happy to have been a part of the successful sale of your house. You can contact us at vick@vicksahotahomes.com, and mamta@vicksahotahomes.com, to share your sales experiences, and also to become part of your success story. Happy selling....

Mamta Sahota & Vick Sahota

ACTION PLAN

_____
_____
_____
_____
_____
_____
_____
_____
_____
_____
_____
_____
_____
_____
_____
_____
_____
_____
_____
_____
_____
_____
_____